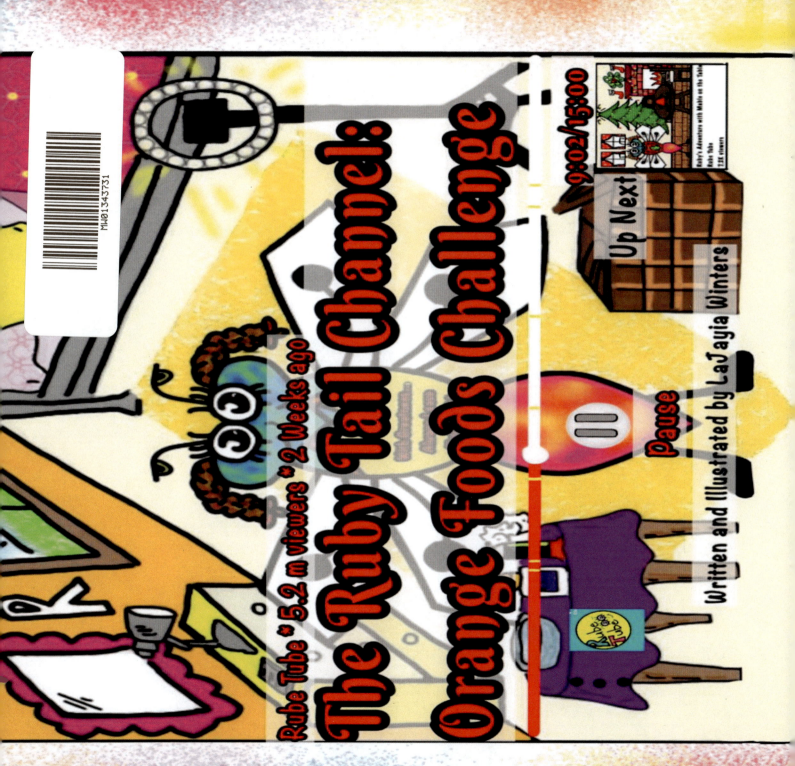

Subscriptions

Read the latest episodes you love!

Sign in now to subscribe to this episode.

Sign In

Copyright (c) 2019 by LaJayia Winters

All rights reserved. There is no allowance for this book or any portion thereof, to be reproduced or used in any manner whatsoever without the express written permission of the publisher, with the exception of a brief quotation in a book review.

Written and illustrated by LaJayia Winters.

Thank you for buying an authorized copy of this work.

ISBN: 978-1-7347832-0-9 (paperback)

Printed in the United States of America

THE RUBY TAIL CHANNEL

A	B	C	D	E	F	G	Delete
H	I	J	K	L	M	N	&123
O	P	Q	R	S	T	U	
V	W	X	Y	Z	-	'	
		Clear	Space	Search			

The Ruby Tail Channel Halloween
The Ruby Tail Channel Mable on the Table
The Ruby Tail Channel Cupcake Challenge
The Ruby Tail Channel Hair Dos and Donts

Ruby's Adventure with Mable on the Table
Ruby Tube Tales
7.2K viewers

Ruby's Halloween Adventure
Ruby Tube Tales
5.7M viewers

Dedications

First shoutout goes to my God for all that He has done! He is truly AWESOME!

Next shoutout goes to my family who had to hear me fuss about the IPad and charger! Lol! Santorrian, Chosia, Chansalee, Chaselynn, and Chandler...you believed in me and helped me along the way. You guys totally rock! I love you!

To my mom, dad, brothers, cousins, family and friends...thank you for the motivation.

Thank you for believing in me. Every "You can do it" has been wrapped and stored in my vault for Ruby's next episode! I love you guys so much!

2 Chronicles 15:7

But as for you...(YEAH YOU!)
Be strong and DO NOT
give up, for your work
will be rewarded.

 Search · Home · Subscriptions · Library files · Account · Settings

You see, I wanted to have a day where I ate only orange foods for 24 hours. I thought it might be easy since I like oranges and carrots a lot. What other orange foods can you think of? Put them in the comments below (or just say them aloud because...well... this is a book!)

So, I woke up early this morning to prepare things for my Wahoo-Tube channel. I noticed that I had only one thing left on my to-do list. This task required the help of my brother Rudy. He has a great eye for finding things.

BANG, BANG, BANG!!!

"Wake up you little stinger!" I yelled as I beat on my brother's bedroom door. "It's adventure time!"

We got dressed, ate breakfast, and begged our mom for permission to go to the nearby store. "Sure, just stay together, keep your phone turned on and be back by noon", she said while giving us the "Mom Look." Yes ma'am, we saluted. We know what the "Mom Look" means...and I bet you guys do too!

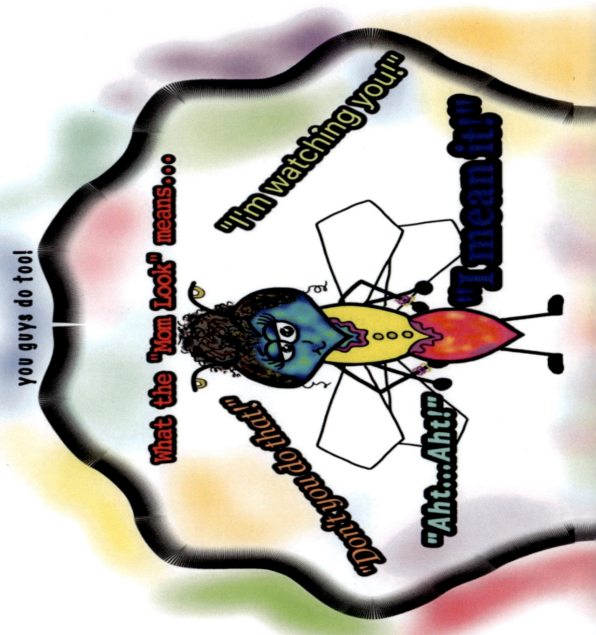

What the "Mom Look" means...
"I'm watching you!"
"I mean it!"
"Don't you do that!"
"Aht...Aht!"

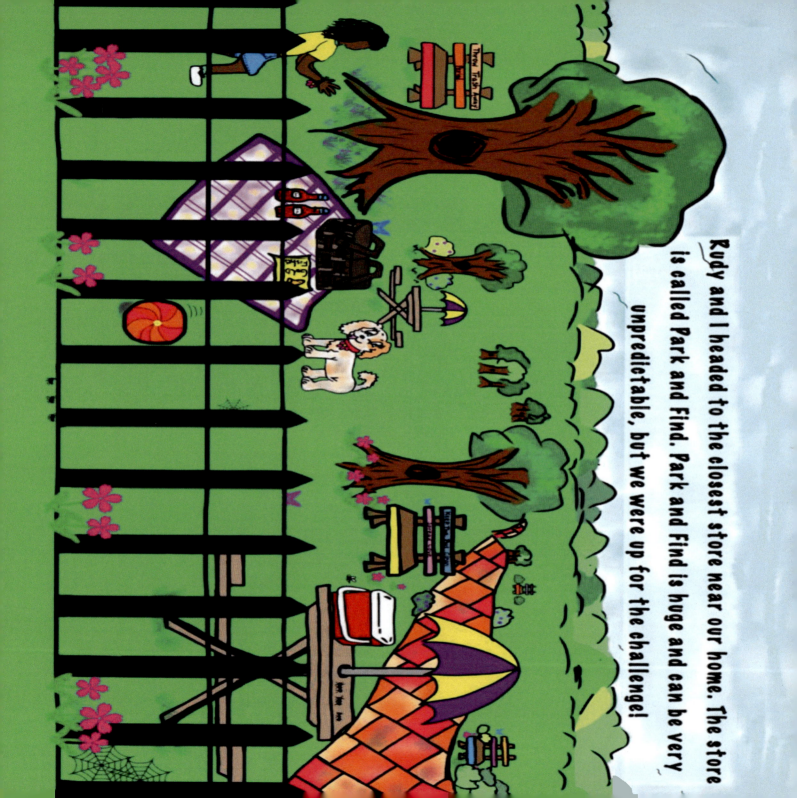

Rudy and I headed to the closest store near our home. The store is called Park and Find. Park and Find is huge and can be very unpredictable, but we were up for the challenge!

"Stay by my side," I told Rudy. "Don't touch anything, and don't ask for anything. We are only here to get what we need," I explained. Those were a few things I've heard my parents say before, and they usually work"!

I grabbed my basket, and we were off!

First stop: Snack Aisle

I know, I know! Don't worry guys, we know having too many snacks isn't good for you and we would only get a few!

Now back to the story.

The store was so busy! I mean...everybody and their mom was there! I thought to myself, "This is going to take a while." But to my surprise, I instantly heard a wonderful word echoing in my ear.

"GOLDFISHIES!!!"

"GOLDFISHIES...
GOLDFISHIES...
GOLDFISHIES!!!

Rudy spotted GOLDFISHIES snack foods, one of our favorites.

You see...this is the very reason why I needed Rudy on this adventure. He's my special helper!

Echoing!! LoL ;)

I quickly flew over to the snacks and tossed a few of them in a small baggy. But just then...out of the corner of my eye; I detected something so delicious and tasty...something as bright as the morning sun!

Woooowwwww!!!!

It was Rudy's favorite candy, Lemon Big Heads! I darted over and swiftly bagged up a few brightly colored candies and put them into the basket. Rudy was going to be so excited, I thought to myself.

But wait... Where's Rudy? Is he lost?

Oh no...

I'VE LOST RUDY!!!

My heart dropped.
What was I going to do?
What was my mom going to say?
But before I could worry myself too much,
I heard a small voice yell out....

"THE FLOOR IS LAVA!!!!!!"

It was from Rudy!

He loves that game, but now isn't the time to play.

BECAUSE.....

This time the floor really was lava!

And it was coming right at us!

AAAAHHHHHHH!!!!!!

We both began to run for our lives!

5...4...

We had to jump over logs.

We even had to dodge an army!

3...2...1!!!!

We finally made it to safe grounds away from the lava.

(At least we thought it was lava, either way...)

"Whew, that was a close one!", I said while trying to catch my breath.

Bad News: I dropped the Goldfishies :(

Good News: We found safety near a unusually warm slime waterfall.

Ps. We bagged some up to play with later! :)

Our Second Stop: Veggie Ground

I know that look, and I know what you guys are thinking. You think that I needed to hear the "Stay Together" speech again. And you may be right!

Our first stop didn't go as planned, but we weren't giving up just yet. We refocused and set our minds on the task set before us. We adjusted our antennas and started our flight.

"I spy with my little eye something orange and crispy," shouted Rudy, seconds into the mission. That's my special helper, alright!

There just awaiting our arrival were freshly cut carrot cubes. Right next to the carrots was a mountain of corn. What luck, I thought! Corn is my mom's favorite vegetable. I decided that we should grab a few kernels of corn to surprise mom with. After all, she always surprises us!

So we set our gears to get ready for landing. When all of a sudden, the weather seemed to start changing. The sky became dark, as if a shadow man was coming after us. Little water droplets began to quickly fall upon us!

This was bad, VERY BAD!

We were in the middle of a storm and we needed a plan...FAST!

But what could we do?

Yeah, you guessed it! We had to break the "Stay Together" rule and split up!

"Rudy, I need you to go that way, swoop down and grab a few pieces of corn; while I go this way and grab the carrots," I commanded.

"Yes ma'am," he called out.

We revved up our engines, zoomed down, and collected the vegetables. Just when I thought that we were in the clear, a large downpour of rainfall blasted me! It was so strong that I wasn't so sure it was rain anymore.

But whatever it was...I was DRENCHED! What was worse...I dropped the carrots.

Things weren't looking good. We didn't have anything for the orange foods challenge. There was no time to go back, plus it was way to dangerous. But on a good note; Rudy was able to grab the corn for mom, and we still had enough time left for one more stop. We weren't giving up that easy!

Our Last Stop: Refrigerated aisle

We flew directly into the refrigerated section, where Rudy quickly spotted fruit.

"Magic oranges!" He pointed out.

He's so cute! He has always called mandarin oranges, magic oranges. And those eyes! I keep telling you guys that he has the best eyes! That's why he's my special helper!

So, without delay, we zoomed over to bag up the oranges and placed them into my basket. Near the oranges were some delicious looking pineapples. I added a few pineapple chunks into the basket since they were our dad's favorite.

No sooner than when I closed the lid of the basket, I noticed something....Rudy was no longer by my side! NOT AGAIN!!! I looked around but there was no sight of him. Then I heard a strange sound... SPLISH, SPLASH, SPLAT!!!!!!!

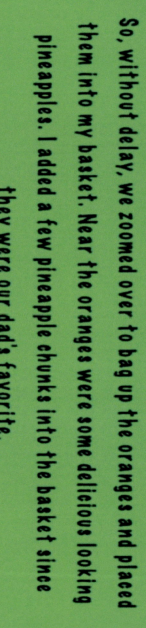

I FOUND HIM...IN THE FREEZER!!!!

He was stuck on an iceberg! OMG!!!
What was I going to do?

I flew to Rudy's aide and tried to help him off the ice, but I wasn't strong enough. I caught sight of a family of ants who was shopping nearby and asked for their help.

Without any questions, they scrambled together, forming a line. They linked to one another like a chain. They grabbed around me tightly with a rope as I pulled Rudy. With one big pull.... POP!!! We went flying through the air and tumbled to the ground. This had been one crazy day, but at least Rudy was safe.

As we thanked the ants, my Bee-Phone started to ring! "BUZZ...BUZZZZ." It was our mom. "Hurry home Ruby, I have a surprise for you two," she said. I grabbed Rudy's hand to keep him near me. I looked at the time on my phone; it was almost noon. I picked up my basket and noticed that I no longer had the oranges. With all of that action, the oranges must've fallen out of the basket. I looked at the time again and then back at the basket.

My dad is so funny!

WE DIDN'T HAVE ANYTHING ORANGE!

I glanced at Rudy and thought about trying to go out for one more mission. But then I remembered...

THE MOM LOOK!

"I think it's time we head home," I told Rudy. "We didn't get exactly what we wanted today, but we didn't give up, and that counts for a lot," I said. And we headed home to see our surprise!

We got home by noon so mom didn't give us "The Look". Our parents greeted us at the door with smiles. Their smiles became even bigger when we showed them the goodies we had in the basket for them. But no one was smiling bigger than Rudy when he saw his favorite candy!

Our day got even better when mom gave us our surprise...

**FRENCH FRIES!!!!
OUR FAVORITE!!!!**

Well, that's it for story time today guys! WHAT A DAY! I hope you will tune in when we eat our yellow foods. If you enjoyed today's episode give us a BIG thumbs up! Go ahead...do it right now, I'll wait!

BUT FIRST... It's time for the 5-second challenge! Tell me your favorite part of this episode in 5-seconds 5,4,3,2,1...Done!

Awesome! I want to thank you guys for watching (well actually reading, LOL) and I'll see you for the next challenge. Until then, remember: Internet safety first, ALWAYS be kind, NEVER have fear, because you have POWER, LOVE, and a STRONG MIND! Peace!!

Made in the USA
Middletown, DE
18 January 2021